Public Speaking

Finicky's 7 Essential Steps Used By Top Entrepreneurs

By Simon Roche

Finicky Inc.

New York

About me

Hi, my name is Simon Roche, Founder of "Finicky.us" and also the author to many entrepreneurial and self-help books.

I have seen that I was different since I was a kid. When other kids wanted to play, I wanted to be productive and better myself. Not to say that I didn't play on my free time, I just didn't play longer than I needed. I always set my expectations out of my reach and I truly hope that my readers do the same. I have visited many companies during my career and I can say that I have learned more than if I were to have worked for a company.

As a thank you for considering my book, I will provide you with one of my many experiences while visiting a friend at Google. My friend who was previously the "Strategic Partner Lead" at Google has had many accomplish through his career and no longer works at Google. We became friends in our marketing course and have still kept in contact.

He gave me a tip about the process of hiring people for my company. During the selection process, he weaves out many strong candidates. Why? Simply because they aren't smarter than me, the interviewer. He explains that if you want a good company, then you surround yourself with average brains that just want to get by. At Google, we don't want average, we want the smartest. Smart people hire smarter people and that's how Google is still on top of its industry. He stated, "I want to hire someone who is smarter than me, works better than me, and is more innovative than me. That way I will be happy when they take my position, as I move on to another chapter in my life"

Through my books, I will share many of my unique experiences and will provide you with mistakes that I have made myself as an entrepreneur.

Words from the Author

Before you start reading this book, I will need you to keep a thought in mind.

"To be able to sacrifice what you are, for who you will become"

In other words, if you put aside your excuses, you will get the results you have always wanted. It's time to make a decision. You can choose to stay the way you are or you can decide to take steps towards change.

No one is stopping you from where you want to go, the only person that is stopping you is YOU. Remind yourself every day of who you want to be, and remember to make the right decisions towards your goal. One way to keep your goals set is by checking up on yourself at the end of each week. Set a goal for 2 pounds each week, and by the end of the month you will have cut 8 pounds. Keep your short-term goals small so that it is achievable, but keep your long-term goals big, so that there is no ceiling towards your success.

Chapter 1: How to Present Yourself

Step 1-

The feeling of nervousness or stage-fright when presenting to an audience is perfectly normal. Even the best public speakers still get nervous. This is a part of being human, we are wired to be worried about our reputation and public speaking is a threat to us. In psychological terms, our fight or flight responses comes into play and our body starts feeling different.

Before I go on any further, I would just like to tell you that the fears of public speaking are not to be overcome, we need to adapt to our public speaking environment. I would like you to keep this in mind as you continue to read on. Before considering speaking in public there are some things you must be aware of. The first thing you should do is to find out who you are and what you need.

The feedback you will receive after speaking in public is relevant for what you are going to do next. You should always meditate and answer these questions: Who am I? What do I want? What do I need?

The next thing you need to know is who your audience is.

Besides age, sex, religion or nationality, a public speaker must always know what his audience is expecting from him and he/she must also know how to connect to the audience in an organic way.

Another important thing you should know about public speaking is that it also involves amplifying your gestures.

Public speaking is when your audience represents more than 5-6 people. When you have a large audience you amplify your voice and your body language. You may find a simple gesture to be exaggerated or even ridiculous, but your audience may see it as a very natural thing. There are many exercises that can help you with this aspect.

Your speech and your emotions are very important when speaking in public. Emotions are absolutely necessary because it will control the audience's attention.

Public speaking is all about the speech.

You must practice your speech a lot because this will make it perfect. An actor who appears 20 minutes in a play will practice about 3 months in order to get it right. This is a rule that a public speaker must also take into consideration.

Public speaking also involves a lot of jokes and humor.

A good joke could be the key to your success because your audience will recognize that this is not strictly an information session. You wouldn't want to watch a bland hour-long speech, and neither does your audience.

However, if the audience does not understand your jokes, your speech will be compromised. Therefore, if you have no humor you should avoid making jokes.

Chapter 2: Understand the Basics of Public Speaking

Step 2-

We are more afraid of talking than of dying! It is a strange statement but, unfortunately this is a cruel reality in today's society whether we accept it or not. We talk every day to our family, to our colleagues and yet, many of us have problems with public speaking. The fear of embarrassment, the possible repercussions in case of failure or the lack of experience can make us run away from such an experience.

In reality, all the secrets of public speaking are in us. Beyond all the attributes that professional speakers need to have you also need to follow some steps in order to successfully speak in public and to overcome stage fright.

Basic secrets of public speaking

1. You can choose one or more friends you really trust and ask them to listen to you and then give you a feedback.

Friends are the ones who will not only tell you what they find wrong about your speech but they will also exaggerate a bit in order to be sure that all your mistakes are discovered. Even if it hurts to hear things that you don't agree with, this is a good way to find out what you need to improve.

2. Study famous public speakers.

This will show you how to act in front of an audience and maybe even what jokes to use in order to create an atmosphere. You will understand that it is very important to make people comfortable in your presence when trying to speak in public.

3. Leave your image to professionals

Self confidence comes from the way you look. That is why you should consider investing in a professional hairstylist and in a lot of tasteful outfits. When we enjoy the way we look, our attitude and the power of concentration also improves.

4. Don't complicate things: don't use phrases that are hard to remember

Simple is better and less is more. Keep this in mind when trying to become a master in public speaking. Nobody wants to find out how many complex words you can use in a single phrase.

After all, the purpose of a public speech is to reach ones' soul and in order to do that you have to use simple and strong phrases.

5. Create a story.

Even if it seems a bit hard to believe, we all remember stories. We all remember some stories from our childhood, stories about friends, colleagues, celebrities and so on. A story will gather all the information in an easy context.

6. Don't think about the consequences

We often refuse to talk in public because we are afraid that we'll embarrass ourselves. We forget that our audience is represented by people who are curious to find out what we have to say. The public may not agree with our ideas but if we don't expose them it's like they don't exist.

Chapter 3: **How to Prepare for a Speech**

Step 3-

Advice for shy people

How to get rid of the fear of speaking in public?

How can you overcome the fear of speaking in public?

This fear is a real problem and the way it manifests is very similar to panic attacks. Before speaking in public but also during the speech you get cold chills, you can't control your hands and you look terrified, your voice trembles and you can't remember what you wanted to say.

Did you find yourself in this kind of situation? Then, it is time to take matters into your own hands and do something about it. You can treat your fear of speaking in public with a lot of exercise and training. You have to make some efforts if you want to become a master in public speaking. Follow some simple advice and learn how to speak in public.

In order to overcome your fear of speaking in public you must prepare thoroughly.

You may not be a natural public speaker or you might not have a lot of great ideas or you must also face stage fright but that doesn't mean that you can't change all that. You need to deliver your first public speech and this might frighten you but this is not the end of the world. You must prepare your speech very well. Prepare at least one week before the speech in order to make sure that you will do a great job. Make your text as logical as possible. Also, it is very useful to set some examples and some stories that may help you support your ideas. Practice all this out loud until you feel that you master your speech. You can even record yourself at home if you are facing a very important speech. Try to do everything possible to reduce the fear.

Think about what your audience wants to hear.

A bored audience will react to this and it might make you feel even more afraid and emotional. In order to avoid this unpleasant moment you might consider thinking about the information that your audience wants to hear. Give them some interesting news or some unique solutions to their problems. The main thing is to give them what they want!

Consider your speech as the most important role of your life

All in all, public speaking is just an artistic show and this might even be an advantage for you even if you are not a professional actor. Costume parties are a real success because people get to feel free while dressing up and talking to others behind a mask. This is an aspect you should consider when talking in public. Imagine that you must act and forget all about your inhibitions. The situation resembles the one in which you are having a glass of red wine and you start to feel relaxed. Just remember not to actually have a glass of wine before giving a speech in front of a real audience!!!

Benefit from your strengths

You have a great sense of humor which brought you a lot of compliments over the years? Then, it's time you use it in a very beneficial way! On the other hand, if you don't have a sense of humor you must remember not to make inappropriate jokes in the key moments of your speech. However, you can tell an interesting story that only you know and that is related to the topic of your speech.

Check out very well the room you will speak in

Another useful advice is to check the place you are about to speak in. It won't hurt to practice your speech there and to sit in the chair in from the stage. This will also allow you to use your imagination and to visualize the audience. This idea is often used by musicians before major concerts and it will help you diminish the fear you feel while speaking in public.

Chapter 4: **Use Your Body to Communicate Your Thoughts**

Step 4-

You can learn how to use your entire body as an instrument that can provide a lot of power to your speech. As a public speaker, you are the most important visual element for your audience. Here are some reasons why you should be considered important as a public speaker:

You don't need to change the light in the room in order to be seen

You don't get stuck

You don't make a fool of yourself

You don't need a technician to follow you around

You don't depend of anyone else

The development of your public speech begins with an exam of the nonverbal message you send to your audience. This includes:

A proper posture

Gestures

The way you move

Facial expressions

Eye contact

The way you dress.

When presenting a public speech, the people who are watching you use their eyes and their ears but also their instincts in order to determine if:

You are honest

You are really opened to the idea of speaking in public

You are interested in your audience and you care about the people that are listening to you

You are confident and in control

Your actions are worth more than your words

Take into consideration the following examples. A person gets on a stage while rearranging his notes. He grabs in a very powerful manner the desk he will sit at and he begins his speech by saying: "It is a great honor for me to be here today and I want you to know that I have a very important message to deliver you." The effect that such an opening line might have can be anything but positive. The public speaker transmitted the contrary through his/her body language. That public speaker actually said: "I am very uncomfortable and I don't really want to be in this place right now."

The visual message that this person transmitted could be a result of his/her nervousness and the lack of experience or simply a physical discomfort that was transmitted in an unconscious way. His/her nonverbal communication described him/her as an incompetent, as a dishonest or indifferent person. Perhaps this person is not really like this but it doesn't matter.

When you speak in public, your audience tends to feel your attitude from the moment you get on the stage. For example, if you are not enthusiastic, your audience will feel the same thing. If you are emotional, your audience will probably be emotional as well. If you don't find your place on that stage, your audience will perceive this as a lack of control or as if you doubt what you are about to say. That is why it is very important that you express exactly what you are feeling. Your body language must not "work" against your goals.

Here are some benefits of an appropriate body language:

Your actions may give more importance to the message you want to deliver.

People tend to get bored of things that are not moving. They will look at some objects that move.

The audience can remember the messages that have multiple meanings. Therefore, simple gestures, the movements of your body or your facial expressions are valuable tools when used in a very intelligent way.

Your actions can emphasize the ideas you are trying to present. The written language includes commas, question marks, and exclamation points. However, when you talk you can use a set of "symbols" that help you emphasize the most important part of your speech.

Your actions can actually help you get rid of stress. It is perfectly normal to be nervous before speaking in public because this means that your speech is important for you but proper use of body language can make all those emotions disappear once you start talking.

3 tips that can give help you when speaking in public

Use humor

This tip is only recommended for people with a real sense of humor. If you know that you don't have what it takes, it is best not to try because you can ruin your presentation. Everything must be as natural as possible.

Use information and quotes from newspapers and magazines

Find articles that are related to your subject. Try finding an interesting story told by someone or the results of a certain research and include that information in your presentation.

Add questions to your presentation.

If you ask questions your audience will think more about what you are saying. Try using the 5W rule: who, what, when, where, why.

Here are some examples:

-"How many of you believe that talking in front of a large group of people is easier that talking in front of a smaller group?"

- "What do you feel when talking in front of a large group of people?"

You can prepare these questions in advance and you can ask them directly to the group or to each person from the audience.

Chapter 5: **Principles of Public Speaking**

Step 5-

Here are the main principles you need to follow when talking about public speaking. These principles are very important and without them, your public speech my turn out to be a disaster.

The first person you need to convince is yourself. This is a mistake that public speakers make at class and at certain events. They are not convinced that their ideas are good and they might not convince the audience either. A good public speaker must learn to speak from the bottom of the heart because it is very important that your ideas get to the audience both on an emotional and rational level. If the ideas you present are not interesting you need to give your speech in a more emotional way. Which part of your speech can really touch your heart? Every idea has at least one part that can be presented in an emotional way. Choose to present only that part. Less is more and this is available for everything not only for your speech.

Understand that it is a big difference between what you "deliver" to your audience and "how you deliver it". If you are really a professional it doesn't necessary mean that you are a master in public speaking. This is a trap that many experts fall into because they train very much to know the information they need to deliver but they forget about the way they deliver it. This is a huge problem because the whole information you deliver to the audience only contains about 7% verbal facts and. The rest is about the nonverbal message. Let's take sports for example. Take a talented athlete who is not practicing enough and compare him to a less talented one who practices a lot. Who do you think wins? The second one will win. Why? He will win because he is more focused on "how" to win.

Expect the best things but get ready for the worse. It is very important to see things in a very positive way and to consider that the audience only came to see you and to listen to what you are about to say. If we take into consideration the main principle of Pareto we find out that only 20% of the audience seek for mistakes while the rest hope they will learn something. It is also very important to have a plan B at hand just in case. A good speech means that you must take into consideration every possible reaction of the audience and to have a response for each situation.

Begin your public speech with the end and ask yourself what is the message you want to send to your audience. Build your speech starting from the end and not vice versa. Van Gogh used to say: "I dream about my paintings and then I paint my dreams."

Enjoy every moment of your speech just as you enjoy each moment of your life. Your speech is a part of your life. The way you prepare it must be the same way you prepare many moments from your life. Consider this before speaking in public!

Chapter 6: What Does the Audience Want to See?

Step 6-

You can convince your audience to listen your speech if you opt for some special techniques used by famous public speakers all over the world. Don't make any mistakes. The ability to sell your ideas is the only one that can help you reach your goals. Follow some valuable public speaking lessons and your audience will be inspired and mesmerized by you.

1. Show your passion. Passion leads to perfection and this is exactly what you are looking for when speaking in public.

You will not be able to inspire others if you are not inspired. You need to create an enthusiastic, passionate and meaningful connection between the subject of your speech and your audience.

2. Use storytelling. Use stories to reach people's minds and souls. Stories will stimulate the human brain and they will help you to connect with your audience.

3. Teach people something new. People are attracted to everything that's new. If you include an unusual or an unexpected element in your presentation you will provide your

audience the possibility to see the world in a different way. An explorer who participated at the search of Titanic in 1985 used to say that "the goal of any presentation is to inform, educate and inspire. You can only inspire people if you give them new ways to see the world in which they live."

4. Surprise your audience in an emotional way. Make sure that your presentation cause powerful emotional responses. You need to make your audience feel joyful, afraid, shocked or surprised. These kinds of feelings will draw your audience's attention and will be remembered long after the public speech is over.

5. Use humor without telling a joke. As mentioned before, humor can make your audience more receptive to what you are saying. Humor also allows you to be seen by your audience in a pleasant way. People are willing to listen, to support and to do business with people they like. Did you know that you can make people laugh and that you can make them like you even without telling a joke? Sir Ken Robinson is a very well known public speaker that delivers his speech this way. One of his most famous speeches is called "How can school kill creativity". Robinson speaks in a very funny way about this field. He says that "If you are attending a festive dinner and you say that your field of expertise is education – actually if you work in this field you can't really get invited to festive dinners." Robinson makes very strong observations that challenge people to try encouraging children's creativity using

some humorous anecdotes. These anecdotes bring him closer to his audience.

6 .Respect the 18 minutes rule. A good public speech should only last about 18 minutes. This should be enough to expose your point of view. Also, some important researchers in the field discovered that too much information can deform the point of the speech. They also discovered that 18 minutes is enough time to deliver your message in a serious and short way.

7. Images are more important than texts. PowerPoint is not your enemy while bullet points are. The most successful speeches are the ones delivered in PowerPoint, Apple Keynote or Prezi but you should never include bullet points. You should always use images, animations and you should avoid long texts. This technique is based on the superiority of images and on the fact that an idea is better presented when it's accompanied by a good image.

8. Be yourself. The most inspired public speakers are opened, authentic and sometimes they are even vulnerable. Many important specialists in the field talked about vulnerability and the way it can help you know yourself and your audience.

Chapter 7: Choose an Idol and Learn From Them

Step 7-

We have talked a lot about what public speaking is, about what to include in your speech, about how to get over your fear. A good public speaker can understand better all these mentioned above if he/she studies more about famous public speakers. Here we can find people like Steve Jobs, Tony Hsieh, Chris Rock, Bill Clinton or Dr. martin Luther King jr.

Follow the example of a great man called Steve Jobs.

Every time we think about really good public speeches we think about the brilliant and successful one held by Steve Jobs at Stanford in 2002. By analyzing it we can identify some key points that draw the audience's attention, sympathy and fascination.

Synchronize with the audience. Steve Jobs knew how to balance his speech and how to adjust it depending on the audience's reaction. He used to wait for people to finish applauding, he knew how to make a pause at certain times and he never gave hasty answers. By using eye contact, he could "diagnose" his audience's state of mind and he could react to it. For example, if the audience laughed he used to continue his speech in a very happy way. However, you must be careful not to exaggerate.

Summarize the content of the presentation but don't tell it. There are public speakers that make the mistake of describing in a detailed way each aspect of their speech. This is very boring! You should rather stick to two or three short sentences such as: "To begin with, I have some news for you. After that, well continue with... So, let's begin!" That's what Jobs used to do.

Use a catchy introduction if the subject allows you. Don't hesitate to start your speech in a very spectacular and captivating way. Sometimes you can even relate your speech to a personal experience. For example, if you are going to talk about emotions you can start by telling your audience a short personal event that can cause a powerful reaction. Steve Jobs included in his speech at Stanford the story about the father he never met. It is important to give something to your audience without getting to far from the subject. If you don't respect this rule your audience may find you a bit too dramatic.

Be emotional yet rational at the same time. Connect to your audience in a rational way. For example, if your audience is made of teenagers you can try using an appropriate language in order to create a friendly atmosphere. Distribute your emotions and your jokes so that you remain true.

Talk to your audience not to your slides. Even if you have some interactive slides to use in your speech this doesn't mean that you need to talk to them. You need to focus your eyes on your audience and you have to use your slides only to make a bigger impression. Jobs was great at this and this is yet another reason why he is an icon in terms of public speaking.

Never forget about Martin Luther King Jr.

Martin Luther King jr. was another important figure of public speaking. He was truly impressive not only because he was a very good public speaker but also because he was a great leader. In his famous speech called "I have a dream", Martin Luther King jr. taught people to act through the power of words. He managed to set an agenda, a well established purpose and he directed he crowd to a certain goal.

His speech represented a solution for all black people who followed him. Even if you don't join a revolution it is very important to be aware of the fact that a good speech needs that certain calling. If your speech doesn't have a purpose it only represents a beautiful poem.

Tony Hsieh is a great example as well.

Another great source of inspiration for those who want to become masters in public speakers is the CEO of Zappos, Tony Hsieh. He is considered to be an entrepreneur who brought the youthful spirit into the business world. His speeches and his vision about leadership are very complex. Tony brings the art of conversation to his presentations.

He talks to people in a very friendly way; he invites them to "have a cup of coffee with him". Because of these techniques, the audience is opened to his messages. That is what you need to do in order to gain your audience's attention. Don't tell them fairytales. If you involve your audience into your speech you will receive only positive results.

You can't get it wrong if you follow the example of Chris Rock.

Chris Rock is another public figure that might inspire you to become a better public speaker. This actor is a live legend of comedy. He is very well known for his crazy stand-up shows and for the movies he made. We mentioned before that humor is very important when talking about public speaking. Humor is a very powerful way of attracting audience and Rock knows that very well. He often uses jokes to send his message. He is a very dominant yet amusing character. Follow his example and take humor into consideration when speaking in public.

Bill Clinton is a great public speaker. Another good example of a big public speaker is Bill Clinton. The 42nd president of America is seen as a speaker and a great leader. One of Clinton's biggest qualities is his ability to tell stories. When he speaks in public, Clinton always connects to his audience and makes it part of the story. If you choose to treat your audience this way you will see how well received you'll be.

Each speaker has his/her unique way of telling stories and because of that you should always be yourself. However, it is very important to keep in mind all those presented above and you should use all these in your future speeches.

You will soon become a master in public speaking and everyone will listen to what you have to say. You can become the next icon in this field.

BIG Bonus from the Author

I want you to thank yourself for wanting to change and I hope you walk away inspired or smarter.

As you read on you will find tips used by entrepreneurs, and motivational thoughts that come from coaches and entrepreneurs themselves. Have Fun and good luck with your endeavors. Before moving on, I just want to remind you that we are all born on this earth as equals. Some may have more support than others, but we can only characterize ourselves by our own actions. In other words, everyone in this world has potential hidden in a box. Some choose to find a way to open it, and some just leave it there.

Think about this and try to figure out who you are.

Some may be okay living an average life, but then there are also others who constantly look for better.

Life Hacking Tips Used by the Entrepreneurs!

Coffee Nap

This method provided is called, "Caffeine Nap", where you drink a cup of coffee and nap for 15 minutes. The 15 minutes gives you time to rest and allows the caffeine to travel through your gastro-intestinal tract. This will provide you with a refreshing reboot by the time you wake up. But don't go over the 15-20 minutes limit or else you'll wake up in a sleepy state.

Plan the Night Before

You heard of this before, you can either work hard or work smart. It's your choice. There's nothing wrong about working hard, but what's the point of working hard if the results are not there. You need to work smart and change up your routine so that your work is actually effective. Tonight before you go to bed, plan out your work for the next day so that you don't waste time in the morning. Don't waste your mornings on planning out what you want to work on as you are wasting your brains fuel. Your brain is packed with fuel from last night's rest, so go use it on something productive. Don't be like the majority of people who sit on their desk wondering what they need to do. Hope this helps!

Acknowledge Your Accomplishments, But....

You have one win in your hand, but that's not enough. It's not time to celebrate just yet. This is only a small win towards your goal. If you celebrate now, you might just lose the fire that you've always had in you to pursue your dreams. So when you reach a goal, recognize it. Please do so as it will be your source of motivation. The motivation that tells you, maybe it is possible. Maybe this dream isn't out of my reach. Just remember to set your goals high and when you do reach them, set them even higher the next time.

Must Always Take a Break

Remember to Take a Break From Work
-TOTD #4

Health is Wealth

Most of us work for a living, and sometimes we work so hard that we feel too tired to spend time with the people we love. Just remember that our work will always change, but our family will always be there. On another thought, we need to take breaks during excessive periods of work, so that we can replenish our thoughts. Take a walk and get some fresh air.

Motivation for Those Who Want to Succeed

Are You Committed?

You Can Achieve Anything
If You Are Committed

Health is Wealth

Are you interested or are you committed to achieving your current goals? Most may ask, what is the difference? If you have interest in fulfilling your goals, then you will complete your task and never look back. In other words, you will do things the same way as how most people do it. However, if you are committed to your situation, then you will find yourself working more than you need to, and trying to improve your current goals, although they are already good enough. Successful entrepreneurs are successful because they have a purpose behind their tasks, it is more than just interest.

So just ask yourself, are you interested or are you committed to what you are currently doing.

There Should Never Be a Plan "B"

If You Concentrate And Exploit The Weaknesses Of Plan A, There Will Be No Need For A Plan B.

Health is Wealth

You've all heard of Plan B's. They are there to back you up just in case Plan A doesn't work. But what's the point of spending half your time on Plan A and half your time on Plan B. Instead, use your time to focus solely on Plan A so that you can perfect it. A perfect plan is better than two average plans. I've always grown up being told "If you do it right the first time, you won't have to do it a second time". So why do it a second time, you're just wasting energy. Perfect your 1st attempt so that you can move on and accomplish other things in life.

Become a Warrior

Rough Times Are Going To Come,
But They Have Not Come To Stay.
They Have Come To Pass.

Health is Wealth

It's not like we're never going to get hurt in life.
And it's not like these episodes are meant to
devastate us. These harsh times are just the
flow of life and everyone gets them, we just
need to do our part and accept them. It may
sound easy but it really isn't. To accept tragedy
or a mishap in your life is going to be hard
because we're humans. We're emotional and
that's understandable, but what about life. Life
isn't going to wait for you, it's like a train with
no brakes. The Sun is still going to shine, and
the Moon is still going to glow. So try not to
mourn for too long. These hard times are
bound to come, but they have not come to stay.
They have come to pass.

A Forgotten Lifestyle

Live Simply,
So That Others
May Simply Live

Health is Wealth
healthiswealth.us

This is probably going to be my favorite for a while. Live simply, so that others may simply live. A simple saying that would do wonders for the world. In a world where capitalism is King, we often get carried away by lavish lifestyles that we envy of others. There's nothing wrong with treating yourself after a hard day's work. It's just that sometimes we become a bit too selfish. There are many people around us that aren't even able to even eat 3 times a day, and here we are complaining about getting the newest gadgets. Our job to live simply is not going to kill us. We may miss out on getting a few designer handbags or suits, but at the end of the day those funds will allow the unfortunate to live another day.

Stop Waiting and Just Do It

I'll do it later. For some reason we only feel obliged to start working when the deadline is near. Maybe you just need pressure to start working. We all put off work until later and our work becomes faulty when we're done. No time left to correct your mistakes. But that's not how successful people succeed and we need to instill in our minds to organize your workload so that you don't do last minute work.

You Are Only One Person, But...

The Only Way Change
Will Ever Happen, Is If We Speak Up.
Our Words Are Powerful, Lets Make An Impact.

Health is Wealth
healthiswealth.us

This was always my problem. I'm guilty of the, "but I'm just one person" crime. I'm so used to assuming that other people are going to make an effort to change their surroundings that I suppose my input wouldn't make a difference. So what if you're just one person. If you're making a change and people around you see it, then they'll be inspired to make the change with you. You are never just one. There may be many others in the room who have the same idea as you, but are not confident enough to share. Stand up and speak your mind so that confidence may grow in them too. The only way change will ever happen, is if we speak up. Our

words are powerful, let's make an impact.
Don't ever think of yourself as just one.

My Dream Never Faded. Your Doubts Just made it More Clear to Me

They Asked Him, How Did He Do It?
He Replied,
There Was No One Here
To Tell Me I Couldn't Do It

Health is Wealth

Are you sure? No one has ever done it before, so how will you do it? It's Impossible.

Well that's not new. People telling you what's possible and what's impossible. But what do they know. They don't know how much time and effort you put in every day and night into your work. If they tell you that it's impossible, let it fuel your fire. Proving people wrong was always a hobby of mine. So go out there and work. And when that day comes, you could tell your doubters that it was always possible.

Even if no one sees it for you, you must see it for yourself. And just like that you are on the road to success.

How's Your Willpower?

Stop setting goals and stopping half way.
Sometimes we get inspired and decide to
dream big. And after the next day the
inspiration is gone and we decide to quit. The
problem is not that we have set your goals too
high. There's no such thing as setting your
goals too high. The problem is us. If we don't
want it bad enough, then we will be like the
majority of people who start something and
then say it's getting nowhere. Well don't expect
results to come in just a couple of days, this is a
long term commitment. We have to be
committed to what we do in order to get far.
We can start and end half way, but what does
that really say about our willpower. You are
only as good as your weakest day.

We Used to Dream a Lot

When We Were Kids, We Saw Things Differently.
In The Simplest Things Around Us, We Imagined
Endless Possibilities.

Health is Wealth

Back then we used to tie a towel around our
neck and jump off our beds only to soar for a
couple of seconds. But those couple of seconds
were enough to allow us to feel like
superheroes. We turned that towel into a cape
and it gave us an identity. When we were kids,
we saw things differently. In the simplest
things around us, we imagined endless
possibilities. Who would have known that a
chunk of metal would help us fly around the
world? That's absurd right? It's hard to imagine
an airplane from looking at a chunk of metal.
As we grow older we slowly push our
imaginations aside, and that towel that used to
help us fly is just a rag to us now. We've grown

up in a world filled with pessimists, whom only know how to provide doubts into our imaginations. It's hard to be innovative when we have so much doubts in our own ideas. So just let those imaginations come back and give them another chance. You'll never know where those imaginations will take you.

G.R.I.N.D.

Happiness Is Not About Getting What You Want.
It's About Loving What You Have.
So Get Ready It's A New Day.

Health is Wealth

Sometimes I feel like I'm not making any progress toward my goals and it frightens me. My dreams and goals are still there, but I have my doubts like any human would. So today I turned on my speakers and Asher Roth was on. It was only then that I realized that I was doing it all wrong. My goal was to work hard so that I could buy my parents stuff that they would be happy to have. I wanted them to be happy. I wanted them to know that in the near future, their working hours would be lessened and that I would bombard them with gifts.

But it wasn't until today, that I realize how faulty my goals were. I was so focused on spending time on work for a better future that I nearly forgot about spending time with my parents in the present. Spending money on my parents can come a little later, but for now it's about spending time with the people you love. Happiness isn't not about getting what you want all the time, it's about loving what you have. So get ready, it's a new day.

Appreciate What You Have!

Today we are so focused with getting new things that we neglect what we already have. We look forward to creating new relationships, and leave behind the relationships we already have. Instead of trying to fix the problems in our current situations, we look for something new as a solution, but at the end of the day we are just dragging out the problem. So let's fix something today, before looking elsewhere. When a friendship is confronted with problems, they settle the problem with each other and grow stronger together.

Stuck in Your Comfort Zone?

The First Step To Success?
Refuse To Be A Captive
Of Your Environment.

Health is Wealth
healthiswealth.us

You say you want to be healthy. You say you want to be rich. But are you doing anything towards these goals. Surrounding yourself with a room full of junk food is not going to help. Neither is hanging around people who don't believe in working hard. You need to get out of your old environment and go find a new one. Stop being trapped in the misery that is around you. Go meet new friends that actually care about the wellness of their body and people who set new goals every week. Once you are in their environment, you'll find yourself trying to work as hard as or even harder than them. Place yourself in a healthy environment, but first you have to leave your old one.

Thank you for taking the time to read this book and may you always have a perfectly balanced life. If you haven't already read my author's description before purchasing this book, you would know that I am also the founder of Finicky. The images provided by the book come from my website, "Finicky.us"

Preview of "Belly Fat Diet"

You may purchase this book by <u>clicking here</u>

Or by using this link
<u>http://www.amazon.com/Belly-Fat-Summer-Natural-Effective-ebook/dp/B00YLZI7P0/ref=pd_sim_351_7?ie=UTF8&refRID=15M94VG9F5F78NMSM7DH</u>

Let's face it, losing belly fat is no walk in the park, it is really, really hard and with summer time around the corner, the pressure to fit into our swim suits is on. Most of us relish the thought of sun bathing on white sandy beaches, sipping on our favorite cocktails. But sadly, the bulge gets in the way of this dream. Now, it is important to note that belly fat is not merely a wardrobe malfunction it's much deeper than 'vanity'. Yes, we all want to display washboard abs in your monokini and bikinis but, belly fat is a **MAJOR** health problem.

We all have fat around our major organs that provide cushioning against shocks. The problem comes in when this fat (visceral fat)is too much as it can now interfere with how our organs function and result in serious health conditions such as heart disease, diabetes, cancers, stroke and so on. This is one of the reasons why you need to work on your tummy.

We also want to help kick start your journey to your ideal body with this 10 day program that will leave you feeling better than ever before. Whether you are doing it for 'vanity' or health reasons, what I can guarantee you are immense confidence and happiness once you complete this 10 day program, which of course doesn't end there!

As for the second question, most of us can attest to following at least one diet plan that may or may have not given us the results we were looking for. You may have had of the 80/20 rule: